RESILIENCE

RESILIENCE

PROTECTING YOUR BUSINESS FROM DISASTERS IN A DANGEROUS WORLD

ROBERT A. COLLINS, PH.D.

iUniverse, Inc.

New York Lincoln Shanghai

Resilience

Protecting your Business from Disasters in a Dangerous World

Copyright © 2007 by Robert A. Collins

iUniverse books may be ordered through booksellers or by contacting:

iUniverse
2021 Pine Lake Road, Suite 100
Lincoln, NE 68512
www.iuniverse.com
1-800-Authors (1-800-288-4677)

Because of the dynamic nature of the Internet, any Web addresses or links contained in this book may have changed since publication and may no longer be valid.

The information, ideas and suggestions in this book are not intended as a substitute for professional advice. Before following any suggestions contained in this book, you should first consult your accountant or other financial advisor. Neither the author nor the publisher shall be liable or responsible for any loss or damage allegedly arising as a consequence of your use or application of any information or suggestions in this book.

ISBN: 978-0-595-40924-2 (pbk)
ISBN: 978-0-595-85287-1 (ebk)

Printed in the United States of America

Contents

Acknowledgements

This book comes out of the experiences of living through Hurricane Katrina in New Orleans. During this period I was able to witness many acts of resilience, and I was able to analyze them as a resident of the city, as well as in my professional role an urban planner and social scientist. I would like to take this opportunity to thank several people. Marshall Stevenson, Dean of Social Sciences at Dillard University, has always been supportive of my research and supportive of having an urban studies program at the university. Marvelene Hughes, President of Dillard University, somehow managed to lead the university through the most difficult year of its history and therefore provided an outstanding case study for this book. I thank both of them for their leadership. I would also like to thank Harvard University Design School Dean Alan Altshuler and Urban Planning Department Chair Jerold Kayden. They gave me the opportunity to serve as Lecturer in Urban Planning at Harvard during the semester that Dillard was closed. I am indebted to them for their generosity.

Introduction

Disasters are a natural and predictable part of the human condition. This includes both natural disasters and human-made disasters. In spite of this, whenever a disaster strikes, most people are unprepared. The inevitable result is the loss of life and property. It does not have to be this way.

The purpose of this book is to synthesize the knowledge gained from observations of how corporations, universities, and governments responded to disasters. The successful techniques of responding to disasters are codified in the following "Ten Commandments of Resilience." This text is primarily targeted toward creating resilient business enterprises. However, government agencies, educational institutions, non-profit entities, and even individuals can protect themselves from the massive disruption caused by disasters if they obey these universal principles.

This book was inspired by observing how certain corporations survived and thrived in South Louisiana after Hurricane Katrina. Additional examples of corporate resilience gained from case studies of past disasters were compared to the Katrina case studies in order to determine which characteristics are present in resilient companies. These characteristics are universal and can be applied to any enterprise.

Whenever a company fails after a disaster, inevitably it can be proven that it violated one or more of these commandments.

This book is different from other disaster planning books in one very significant way: while most disaster books focus merely on teaching groups how to survive disasters, this one focuses on teaching people how to thrive and profit from them. Since disasters are an inevitable part of life, the wisest course of action is to understand them, prepare for them, and capitalize on the opportunities that they present.

The Ten Commandments of Resilience

I. Thou Shalt Have a Written Disaster Plan

II. Thou Shalt Do Cost Benefit Analysis

III. Thou Shalt Be Fully Insured

IV. Thou Shalt Search Out and Repair Vulnerable Systems

V. Thou Shalt Have Redundant Systems

VI. Thou Shalt Be Mobile

VII. Thou Shalt Set and Follow Priorities

VIII. Thou Shalt Not Depend on Others

IX. Thou Shalt Keep Lines of Communication Open

X. Thou Shalt Capitalize on Opportunities

Chapter 1

Thou Shalt Have a Written Disaster Plan

The first and most important step in disaster planning is, obviously, to have a plan. Without a specific plan, it will be very difficult, if not impossible, to implement the other steps in disaster preparation. Most organizations deal with disasters by first hoping that they don't happen. Then when they do happen, they respond to them and try to recover from them. Most organizations do not try to mitigate them in advance. This is an irrational and expensive strategy. Yossi Sheffi, Professor of Systems Engineering at MIT, conducted a three year study of resilient organizations from Toyota to UPS to the US Navy, and drew a simple conclusion: A company's ability to return to business depends more on the decisions it makes before a shock hits than those it makes during or after the event (Bernstein, 2006; Sheffi, 2006). According to Sheffi, the terrorist attacks of 9/11 forced him and his colleagues to see a more comprehensive view of risk. He states: "Before that, I thought about it mostly in financial terms—buying insurance against various business risks, buying commodity futures such as oil to hedge against price fluctuations, the use of financial derivatives, etc. In the wake of the attacks, I started looking at all kinds of disruptions, and it became clear that there's a lot more to consider than contingency planning or financial hedging. There are low-probability/high impact events like terrorist attacks that may cause unplanned exits from important markets or even the demise of the unprepared business" (Bernstein, 2006, p. 94).

It is impossible to plan for things that you cannot imagine. Therefore, the first step in forging the resilient organization is to conduct "scenario planning." This requires that leaders of the company imagine the worst case scenario. Many corporations claim that they have plans in place to deal with disasters. However, further investigation reveals that the plans they have in place; usually referred to as "business continuity plans," do not really take into account the worst case. Instead, these plans are designed to deal with the basic garden-variety disasters (rain-induced floods, power outages, factory fires, etc.), not major disasters such as hurricanes, earthquakes, tsunamis, or terrorist attacks. These organizations are unprepared, and when the inevitable disaster strikes, the results are catastrophic for the company, its employees, and its shareholders.

Journalist Geoffrey Colvin (2005) argues: "The events that do the worst damage are the ones no one even conceived of. Exhibit A is 9/11. The idea that a passenger jet might crash into the World Trade Center had been thought of; it was a fairly obvious possibility, especially since a plane had once crashed into the Empire State Building. What no one imagined was the combination of large planes with nearly full fuel tanks plus the impact of the crashes jarring fireproofing from the girders, and how this could bring the towers down. In retrospect, it obviously could have been imagined. It just wasn't" (p. 69).

Journalist Amy Bernstein (2006) points out: "Few issues have morphed as dramatically in the last five years as corporate resilience. That phrase once referred to managing risks that were fairly predictable and relatively easy to insure against: fires, strikes, and economic recessions for example. But all that has changed. A string of catastrophes—beginning with the terrorist attacks on September 11, 2001, and continuing through the bombing of the Madrid railway and the Asian Tsunami in 2004, the blast on the London Underground in July 2005, Hurricanes Katrina and Rita in August and September, and the earthquake that devastated Pakistan in October 2005—has rearranged our concept of disaster preparedness. It's no longer enough for companies to devise a business continuity plan and file it away somewhere. They now have to figure out how to bounce back from the unthinkable" (p.93).

It is necessary for the organization to be honest with itself when completing the scenario planning step in disaster preparation. The task here is not to imagine the worst disaster that the organization thinks that it can handle. The task is to imagine the worst disaster that could possibly strike the company, given its geographic location and individual circumstances. Lee Clarke, a disaster planning expert and professor at Rutgers University argues, "It's not crazy to think about the worst cases" (Judice, 2006, p. E-2).

There are three steps to this process: First, the senior management should take inventory of all of the possible disasters that could possibly strike a given area, depending on the location of the company. Second, the team should have a brainstorming session listing which one of these disasters is the worst case scenario, (not simply the most likely to strike). Finally, a written list should be developed. The list should contain all of the possible disasters that could strike the company. The worst case scenario should be at the top, and a plan should be formulated to allow the company to survive and prosper given the worst case scenario. The specific steps of this plan will take up the remainder of this book.

One of the major problems with most plans is that they do not include contingencies for being away from the office from long periods of time. This was one of the most numerous flaws in disaster plans that were in place in New Orleans prior to Hurricane Katrina. Mark Mayer of Peter A. Mayer Advertising, Inc. in New Orleans, pointed out that although they had a comprehensive plan in place "The plan did not anticipate everything that happened" (Judice, 2006, p. E-2). The company's plan assumed that it would be away from of its office for a maximum of two weeks. However, for most companies it was a month or even several months before they could return to the city.

It is necessary to point out that a plan does not exist until it is written down. When asked, many business leaders claim that they have a disaster plan. However, quite often it only exists in their heads. This is not a plan. The plan must be written down and disseminated if it is to be effective.

Many professional disaster planners complement themselves on the complexity and intricacy of their disaster plans. What they don't realize is that no one will ever read their plans. Most employees of your organization are not experts in disaster planning. No matter how intelligent they are, they will not understand a complicated plan filled with technical jargon because they are not trained in the language of technical planning. Therefore, any successful disaster plan must be simple. It must be written in language that any lay person can understand. Everyone in the organization, from the CEO, to the entry-level staff, to the janitors, must be able to able to understand the plan and follow its instructions to the letter.

It is a rule of war, stated by Field Marshall Helmuth Karl Bernhard von Moltke, that "no battle plan survives contact with the enemy." This is also true of disaster plans. A complex disaster plan that looks great on paper will never survive an actual disaster. During disasters, chaos and confusion are the rule. Employees will not have to the time or ability to concentrate on figuring out a complex plan. Therefore, the plan must be as simple as possible. It is also necessary to have periodic drills to test the plan. The company will never know whether or not the plan will work without periodic testing. In the competitive business environment of today, it is necessary for all corporations to have disaster plans if for no other reason than their competitors are increasingly formulating disaster plans. Rob Dyson, leader of consulting firm Accenture's business continuity practice in North America, says, "Business leaders are starting to get it: 'If I'm going to be competitive and meet the requirements of my stakeholders, to deliver a profit, I have to think through these things. Because any one could bring my company to a halt" (Howell, 2006). Phil Bigge, vice president of business continuity at Countrywide Financial, a $10.5 billion company based in Calabasas, California, points out that, "Regulators, partners and customers increasingly are asking if firms are prepared. So having tested plans directly correlates to getting more business" (Howell, 2006).

CHAPTER 2

THOU SHALT DO COST BENEFIT ANALYSIS

There are always costs associated with planning and responding to disasters. These costs could be anything such as: the time and labor put into developing a plan; the purchase of communications and transportation equipment; or the purchase of insurance. There are also benefits associated with planning and responding to disasters; the chief benefit being that a company will survive and be in an excellent position to capitalize on the opportunities that always present themselves after a disaster.

In a successful business, it is important to understand the relationship between costs and benefits. Obviously, it is necessary for your benefits to exceed your costs. While most people understand that this is true when comparing such business costs as training to benefits such as sales, most people fail to apply this concept to disasters. It is important to spend a certain amount of capital on preparing for disasters. However, a company should not spend more money than it will be receiving in benefits. The only way to know how to balance these factors is to conduct a thorough cost benefit analysis.

Smaller companies can do their own cost benefits analysis. They should take into account such cost factors as: How much will it cost, in terms of time, labor, and money, to put an evacuation plan into place and carry it out? How much will it cost to house your employees at a different location, if necessary? How much will it cost to protect your business from the physical aspects of disaster (stronger construction, higher buildings, etc.)? How much will business interruption insurance cost?

Next, it is necessary to explore the benefits of mitigating the disaster: Revenue that will continue coming in after the disaster, as opposed to revenue lost if the disaster is allowed to close the business. How much will the corporation lose if it is closed for a month? How much at two months? There are also non-quantifiable benefits to consider, such as: allowing your employees to continue to hold jobs and have income to support their families; avoiding the devastating financial losses that are inevitable without a disaster plan; and providing your company the ability to capture a larger market share since many of your competitors will most likely be out of commission.

It is necessary to quantify as many of these factors as possible in order to determine the proper amount to spend on mitigation. One quick point should be made here: almost all companies spend too little on mitigation, very few spend too much.

The cost benefit analysis process can be very tedious and time consuming, however it is the only way to assure the company is getting the proper financial balance. As stated earlier, smaller can companies can do this internally. It is best for larger corporations and institutions to hire external expert advice on cost benefit analysis, since the stakes are much higher. "We highly encourage organizations to conduct a business impact analysis," says Brian Turley, president of business continuity software provider and consultant Strohl Systems. "That will tell the executive team in black and white, 'This is what we stand to lose over a one-to-two day period if this building is not available to us'" (Howell, 2006).

When looking for lessons from Katrina, Journalist Justin Fox (2005) points out: "Katrina is an especially poignant study in risk because the catastrophe was so widely foreseen. The Army Corps of Engineers told anyone who asked that the chance in any given year that a storm would inundate New Orleans was between one in 200 and one in 300. Over the 77 years average American's life expectancy, one-in-200 annual odds snowball to one-in-three. Or try this simple (and oversimplified) cost-benefit-analysis: If the cost of a flooded New Orleans is $100 billion, and the annual chance of that flood is one in 200, then it would pay to spend up to $500 million a year (one-200th of $100 billion) to keep such a flood from happening. It would also more than pay, probabilistically speaking, to undertake a forced evacuation whenever a Category 4 or 5 storm threatened the city. Yet nothing of the sort was done" (p.54).

CHAPTER 3

THOU SHALT BE FULLY INSURED

After many modern disasters, the only difference between those who can rebuild and those who cannot is insurance. In guarding from disasters, this insurance normally takes the form of specific event insurance (such as flood or fire insurance) or general business interruption insurance. If a business cannot afford insurance, it is probably undercapitalized and cannot afford to be in business. Without insurance, even a minor disaster can destroy a business forever. It is true that the various types of business insurance available can be expensive. However, when compared against the possibility of a disaster wiping the business out all together, the decision not to purchase insurance is an irrational one. Certainly, it is necessary to purchase the correct amount of insurance depending on the size and the type of business. This is why the cost benefit analysis discussed in the previous chapter is necessary. A business will not know how much insurance to purchase unless it has first done a thorough cost benefit analysis.

Once the cost benefit analysis has been completed, it is necessary to purchase enough insurance to cover any and all contingencies.

Dillard University, a private historically black university in New Orleans, suffered approximately 400 million dollars in physical damage from Hurricane Katrina in 2006. Its campus was uninhabitable and the university was forced to locate its spring semester operations to the Hilton Riverside Hotel in Downtown New Orleans. In addition to the physical devastation caused to the campus, eighty percent of the faculty members lost their homes. The university was faced not only with housing students and finding classroom space, but housing the majority of the faculty and staff at downtown hotels.

The university was able to meet its obligations primarily because the leadership had the foresight to purchase sufficient amounts of business interruption insurance. This insurance was able to cover a large share of the cost of housing for faculty, staff, and students, as well as the cost of leasing classroom space. Dillard is a small university without the huge endowment of wealthy schools. Had the business interruption insurance not been available, the university's very existence would have been in doubt due to the fact that it had already cancelled its fall semester, which meant no tuition revenue was coming in during the months after the storm. Another semester without tuition revenue coming into the university coffers could have been a death knell.

In addition to the financial devastation to the university, the inability to hold a spring semester would have resulted in the loss of hundreds of faculty and staff jobs, and the interruption in the university educations of over one thousand students. In this case, business interruption insurance was not a luxury. It was an absolute necessity.

In most cases, business interruption insurance is not a luxury. It is a necessity because the very existence of the business enterprise depends on it. The same can be said about fire insurance and flood insurance.

CHAPTER 4

THOU SHALT SEARCH OUT
AND REPAIR VULNERABLE
SYSTEMS

All businesses have strengths and weaknesses. In order to survive a disaster, a business must be able to locate its weaknesses or vulnerable systems. Repairing these systems should be a priority. In the City of New Orleans, it was widely known that the system of floodwalls was vulnerable and could not withstand the storm surge from a category 5 hurricane. In spite of this fact, the floodwall system was never reinforced, due to the fact that it was perceived as being too expensive. This was a serious failure to do cost benefit analysis as described in chapter 2.

As a result of the failure of the government to reinforce a system that was well known to be vulnerable, over 1,000 people died and the city suffered over 200 billion dollars in physical damage. History is full of examples of systems that were known to be vulnerable but were never repaired. These include wooden buildings built too close together (The great fires of London and Chicago), failure to enact building codes requiring earthquake resistant buildings (The great earthquakes of San Francisco and Taiwan), and the failure of both governments and businesses to construct buildings strong enough to withstand hurricane force winds (Hurricanes Katrina and Andrew).

After Hurricane Katrina, smart businesses are not waiting on new laws or government mandates, but are instead repairing their own vulnerable systems. Northrop Grumman, a large defense contractor, has come up with a creative plan to protect its essential employees during a hurricane. Instead of keeping them in one of their vulnerable buildings, about 100 essential employees will ride out storms together on one of the Navy ships the company is constructing. The ships are much stronger than many of the buildings on the 200-acre campus of the Avondale shipyard, according to Lou Hose, the company's emergency director. "One of the lessons that we learned (during Katrina) was you better have a Category 5 structure that you can stay in" Hose said (Judice, 2006, p. E-2).

One important aspect of this commandment is consistency. It is not enough for the disaster planning team to search out and repair vulnerable systems once and then assume that the company is ready for the next disaster. This process must be on-going and pro-active. This is due to the fact that systems are constantly degrading, wearing out, and losing their effectiveness. Also, vulnerabilities are constantly changing. A strength today might become a vulnerability tomorrow. Vulnerable systems can include purely physical assets such as buildings and information technology infrastructure. Vulnerable systems can also include networks where humans interface with technology, such as communication networks, transportation systems, and supply chains. In every case, these systems must be constantly probed, analyzed, and tested for weaknesses. When weaknesses are found, they must be repaired immediately so that the company can stay constantly prepared.

CHAPTER 5
THOU SHALT HAVE REDUNDANT SYSTEMS

In today's business environment, many companies avoid redundant systems. The theory being that redundancy is inefficient and not cost effective. This is a mistake. These companies are extremely vulnerable to any disruptions at all. When a disaster strikes, a company without redundant systems will have to shut down indefinitely, losing profits in the process. A company with redundant systems can simply switch to the secondary system and continue operation. All resilient corporations have secondary systems.

For smaller, self-contained companies, simply having back-up operating systems might be sufficient. This includes a gasoline powered generator to provide power during blackouts and a secondary computer system in a different location to back up files. With larger corporations, however, primary systems become more complex, so redundant systems become more complex.

With companies of all sizes, the most important systems that must be made redundant to survive a disaster are the information technology systems. After the attack on the World Trade Center on 9/11, the world saw the importance if having redundant IT systems. Those companies that did not have fully integrated redundancy were not able to survive. Those that had redundancy were able to be back on line in a matter of days. One such example is financial powerhouse Cantor Fitzgerald. The headquarters of the firm was located on the 105th floor of the World Trade Center North Tower. When the tower collapsed, 658 of Cantor's 1,050 U.S. workers were killed. In spite of the emotional toll of the terrible tragedy, Cantor's employees in the US and Europe worked around the clack to recreate systems in temporary offices in New York, New Jersey, and Connecticut. Cantor uses eSpeed as its backbone trading system. It is built on a dual architecture that replicated all functional systems at the World Trade Center with a Rochelle Park, New Jersey site, and also with a site in London. Because of this built-in system redundancy, Cantor Fitzgerald was ready to resume trading within 48 hours of the first plane striking the World Trade Center (Sheffi, 2006, p. 237).

After hard lessons learned from Hurricane Katrina, a "disaster mainframe," used to back up vital records, is now becoming a necessity with many companies. Liberty Bank in New Orleans was unable to operate its ATM and electronic network for three days following Katrina because the computer programs on which they depended were located in a New Orleans building flooded out by the storm surge. As a result of this lesson, the company now maintains additional mainframes in Baton Rouge and in Philadelphia.

Freeport-McMoRan, a multinational mining and energy company, had its headquarters in New Orleans prior to Hurricane Katrina. It realized early on the importance of moving its computer system out of the city. "In our recollection, there's never been a hurricane in Ohio," said Freeport-McMoRan spokesman Bill Collier, referring to the state to which his company's networked computer system now resides

(Judice, 2006, p. E-2). Large multinational corporations are not the only companies that realize the necessity of backup systems. Members of the restaurant industry, so vital to the tourist-centered New Orleans economy, are putting their own systems in place. Dickie Brennan, owner of Dickie Brennan's Steakhouse and a member of the most famous restaurant family of New Orleans, now maintains a computer server for his corporation in San Diego, California. Whitney National Bank has moved its mainframe computers and servers to Dallas (Judice, 2006, p. E-2).

Although IT redundancy tends to get the most publicity and the most attention in business continuity plans, it is not enough for a business to simply have redundant IT systems. In order to survive a disaster, all vital systems must be redundant. This includes communications systems (discussed in chapter 9), transportation systems, security systems, and for manufacturing industries, supply chains.

The need to have redundant supply chains is especially poignant in today's global economy. Sheffi (2006) points out: "The number of possible disruptions to a global supply chain is endless. Manufacturing can be disrupted directly because of a problem in a plant, a disruption at a supplier's plant, a glitch in the transportation system, a disruption to the communication and information system, or a snag with the customer" (p.14). If a company does most of its manufacturing in-house, the simplest way of mitigating supply chain disruptions is to have a large enough back-up inventory on hand, a "safety stock," preferably stored at a second location, so that the company can withstand short term disruptions (a few days) without losing business. However, for supply chain disruptions that last more than a few days, different strategies are necessary.

If the company's supply chain is short or self contained, the simplest way to mitigate a long term disruption is to have a second manufacturing plant. Tom Oreck, CEO of Oreck Corp, a New Orleans headquartered maker of vacuum cleaners and other household products, has planned for this eventuality. Prior to Hurricane Katrina, nearly all of the company's air purifiers, vacuum cleaners, and other household products were built at a plant in Long Beach, Mississippi, which was in the path of the storm. The facility employs more than 500 people. Although the building was storm proof and survived the storm intact, the company still suffered millions in physical damage to the plant and the inventory and was closed for ten days after the storm. Touring the Mississippi neighborhood after the storm, Oreck realized that the damage to the supply chain could have been much worse. Several blocks away, other manufacturing facilities had been completely destroyed by the storm surge. Oreck learned an important lesson: "We realized that having a single location meant we were carrying a great deal more risk than we ought to. We didn't want to be in a position where a single event could take us out of business (King, 2006, pp. C6-C8). This statement by Oreck is the essence of the correct philosophy that a responsible CEO should have. The bottom line is that the corporation should not be carrying more risk than absolutely necessary and the corporation should put itself in a position where a single event cannot put the company out of business.

The Oreck Corporation mitigated these concerns by purchasing a plant in Cookeville, Tennessee. The new plant makes the same core products as the as the Long Beach plant. Duplication of production ensures that the company's future is not imperiled by a single weather event ever again.

The previous case demonstrates how to deal with supply chain vulnerability if the supply chain is mostly self contained. However, in today's global economy, most supply chains involve many different plants and in some cases, many different countries. In these cases, it is not enough to simply build or purchase a second plant. Companies must incorporate strategies that build redundancy by working with multiple suppliers and by building flexibility into the system through the use of standard, interchangeable parts whenever possible.

The next case is an example of the importance of multiple suppliers. In 1995, an earthquake measured at 7.2 on the Richter scale hit Kobe, Japan. The damage to industry was widespread. However, the damage would turn out to be not only local or national in scope, but global. This was because, at the time, Japanese Industry prided itself on the low cost efficiency of lean manufacturing systems. The Kobe earthquake exposed the vulnerability of this paradigm. Toyota Manufacturing Company purchased most of the brake shoes used in its domestic cars from one source: the Osaka plant for Sumitomo Metal Industries. Although the plant wasn't damaged by the earthquake, it lost gas and water supplies and could not operate. Because Toyota relied on lean manufacturing, it had no inventories of the parts. Also, because Toyota had no other large supplier for this part, the lack of brake shoes halted production at most of Toyota's manufacturing plants all over Japan. Toyota lost production of an estimated 20,000 cars and lost about 200 million in lost revenue as a result of their reliance on one supplier (Sheffi, 2006, p. 19).

In order for a company to build resilience into its supply chain, it must, whenever possible, work with multiple suppliers in different locations, so that the disruption to one supplier will not force the company to cease operations. At worst, it will have to reduce output while relying on a smaller stream of supplies from a secondary or tertiary source, but a resilient company can recover from this inconvenience. Whereas a total forced shutdown could result in the permanent loss of customers and the company may not be able to recover.

Another way to build resilience into a supply chain is to use standard, interchangeable parts whenever possible. If a company relies on one specific part from one manufacturer, then the company relying on the part can potentially be held hostage to the supplier if anything were to go wrong further up the supply chain. For example, if a company builds a car with a specific, customized wheel rim, more than likely, that rim will have to be supplied by one, specific supplier, (and usually at a higher cost). However, if the car is designed to use a standard size wheel rim, then the manufacturer will have the option of simply going to a second supplier if the first supplier is disrupted.

CHAPTER 6
THOU SHALT BE MOBILE

Almost all disasters are place-based, (the exception to this rule being certain types of computer problems that can happen anywhere in cyberspace.) When a disaster strikes, the quickest way to make sure that people and assets are protected is to be mobile. It is true that in most cases a company cannot move all of its assets to another location. But that is usually not necessary. What is necessary is that the vital operating systems of the corporation can be moved so that the company can re-start operations in another location. Obviously, a company's most important assets are its people. So the company should have a plan to move them out of the disaster zone first. In a large corporation, this usually involves having access to housing in advance so that the company can move its employees and families out of the disaster zone. In a smaller corporation, this involves having a specific written plan for all of the employees to evacuate at a certain time and having a pre-arranged time and a pre-arranged location where all of the employees will meet up to begin working again.

Dillard University, described in Chapter 3 when discussing the importance of having business interruption insurance, is also an example of the need to be mobile, even if the institution is something as firmly rooted in place as a university. Most universities in the New Orleans area were forced to cancel their fall semesters as a result of Katrina. In addition to having a highly dispersed student population and a lack of public services in the city, the campuses all suffered major damage. With the help of insurance settlements and around the clock work by construction crews, most of the universities in the New Orleans area were ready to hold their spring semesters when January rolled around. Dillard, however, was not as fortunate. Parts of Dillard's campus are located in a low-lying area of the city and half of its buildings were inundated with 8 to 10 feet of standing water which remained on campus for two weeks. The damage was estimated to be in the neighborhood of 400 million. It was too extensive to repair before the spring semester scheduled for January of 2006. The leadership of Dillard had to make a choice. They could either cancel the spring semester and plan on opening again in the fall when the main campus would be ready for habitation, or they could hold university operations on an alternate site. Canceling the spring semester could have been catastrophic for the university. First of all, the institution would have lost a semester of revenue at a time when the university desperately needed operating revenue. Second, in all likelihood, the majority of the university's students would not have returned to the university. Fearing that being forced to sit out another semester would have delayed their graduation, most students would have transferred to other universities. The university may not have survived the disruption. A university in operation since 1869 would have died.

Fortunately, Dillard's president, Marvelene Hughes, made another choice. She chose to be mobile. It was decided that the university would indeed have a spring semester. Since the main campus was not available and since the majority of the buildings in the city were not available, the university knew it would have to open in the third of the city that was on high ground above sea level and therefore not flooded. After reviewing several sites, the university opened up in January at the Hilton Riverside Hotel in downtown New Orleans. The Hilton's convention and trade show space was converted into classroom space by constructing a series of very large cubicles. Since the university had no dorm space, over 1,000 students were also housed at the Hilton. Since most faculty members lost their homes, some were housed at the Hilton and the remainder who needed housing were housed at the Marriott two blocks away. Dillard also located temporary office space to house essential administrative functions as well as provide cubicles for faculty members. All of the satellite sites were connected by shuttle buses that traveled a circuit between the buildings. The move was successful and the university had a successful spring semester. University campuses are more tied to a sense of place than most organizations. If a university can be mobile, then any organization can be mobile.

Fortunately, it is usually not necessary to move an entire organization to a different location for six months. In most cases just being able to move essential personnel is adequate. Even in this case, lessons were learned from Katrina. Firms that need to keep essential and emergency staff in the area during a storm, such as electrical utility company Entergy Corp. and aerospace company Lockheed Martin, had to address issues related to supporting those employees. Due to lack of safe housing in the disaster zone, Entergy had to house its workers in large tents and supply mobile showers and sanitation facilities. As a result of lessons learned during the hurricane, Lockheed Martin has significantly improved the temporary living quarters for their team of 38 workers who remain in the company's emergency operations center during a storm. This team is called the Ride Out Crew. After Katrina, the emergency operations center was relocated from an exterior wall to a windowless space on the interior of the same building. The new space is larger and has multiple big-screen televisions mounted on the wall, a major improvement over having workers huddled over a few small computer screens. Lockheed already had cameras monitoring the levee, and generators ran the video feed when the power went out. But the company increased video surveillance capability to keep workers from having to go out in foul weather to peer at the rising water. Now they can look at those surveillance cameras and view weather data and maps simultaneously. The speaker phones were improved so workers can talk while muting the background noise. Lockheed also is increasing the supply of essentials for workers at the plant and has pre-established contracts with suppliers to bring more food and water to survive for the long term.

Many other New Orleans businesses also learned the necessity of mobility as a result of Katrina. A local criminal defense lawyer, Donald A. Sauviac, Jr., evacuated the city with his laptop computer, a client file, two research books, and his calendar. When the storm hit, he lost all of his office computers and all client files located in his main office, potentially catastrophic for an attorney. Now he says, "I plan on moving the office away from paper. My plans are to be able to scan all of this stuff into the system, have a laptop and be totally mobile" (Judice, 2006, p. E-2).

While the last chapter mentioned the importance of having redundant systems, it is important to note that redundancy can be combined with mobility in order to increase resilience. The large local law firm of McGlinchey Stafford PLLC, responded to the threat of future storms by setting up a network facility in Dallas that has full remote access capabilities so lawyers will be able to work directly off the same network regardless of their physical location. This does away with the need to conduct the labor-intensive task of scanning and copying vital files prior to an evacuation. In deciding to put the mainframe in Dallas, the firm's executive director, Al Thomas said "Not only did it need to be outside of New Orleans, but it needed to be completely out of the area" (Judice, 2006, p. E-2).

In an effort to be more mobile in anticipation of the next hurricane season, Dillard University has instituted the ultimate protection against disruption caused by a mandatory evacuation; it is called the virtual campus. The university's procedures mandate that if the president of the university calls for an evacuation, all classroom activity is converted to online instruction. This is done by utilizing specialized educational software, such as Blackboard, which is designed specifically for the purpose of online instruction. Online educational software is constantly being perfected with more functionality being added all the time. The most recent versions of the software have real-time video conferencing that can even accommodate online instruction in disciplines previously thought to be limited to face to face instruction, such as art and music. All faculty at Dillard are required to attend Blackboard training sessions and to be proficient in the software.

In response to the need to be mobile during future hurricane seasons, the majority of universities in South Louisiana have instituted some sort of virtual campus plan.

Given the fact that the business versions of the technology used in online classroom instruction are also available to corporations, there is no excuse for any corporation not being able to conduct all essential operations from a remote location.

CHAPTER 7

THOU SHALT SET AND FOLLOW PRIORITIES

When putting together a disaster plan, it will be impossible to protect all activities of the company. Therefore, it is necessary to decide which activities are absolutely necessary for the corporation to keep operating. Activities of lesser importance will probably have to be sacrificed. Once a disaster strikes, it is especially important to set and follow priorities. In the chaos and confusion of a disaster, it is often impossible for managers to set and follow priorities. For this reason, it is necessary that the priority activities of the corporation are identified in advance and written into the plan.

The first priority should be the human assets of the company, meaning its employees. This means that the first step must be the evacuation plan. This might be simple, such as shutting down business early in the day to allow all employees sufficient time to get out of town. Or it might be complex, as in the case of a large corporation that has to keep working through the disaster. In this case, housing and workspace will have to have been already secured and set aside in advance, and plans put in place as to when and where employees will meet up. It is also important to make sure that all department heads have back up numbers and e-mail addresses for all employees.

At the same time as the evacuation plan is being put into place, all of the physical assets of the company must be secured. This includes basic steps such as putting computer equipment and vital files onto higher platforms to protect them from flooding, locking all buildings and putting security measures in place to avoid looting. It also includes more advanced steps such as scanning any vital documents into remote back-up servers and removing and transporting any vital infrastructure or products (proprietary lab formulas, manufactured prototypes, etc.).

In addition to prioritizing steps to be taken during a disaster, it is necessary for companies to prioritize customers. Although the company may have a well executed disaster plan, it is probable that it will not be able to satisfy all customers during a disruption. A plan must be put in place in advance as to which customers will be served first in the case of a disruption. The criteria could be based on the size and profit margin of the customer, the level of vulnerability that the customer will experience if not served, or perhaps the protection of a long term and reliable relationship. The criteria used are not as important as the fact that a standard and reliable set of criteria be used in every case. If this is done, then most customers will understand if they cannot be served right away and this protects long term relationships.

A special note should be made here on planning priorities before a disaster strikes. This book offers many ideas and steps that should be taken to protect a company from disaster. It is unreasonable to expect that every corporation will be able to put all of these steps in place. Putting every suggestion into place would probably be cost-prohibitive and would violate the commandment of conducting cost-benefit analysis. Only the largest corporations will have the resources to implement all of the ideas listed here.

The purpose of providing steps and ideas in this book is to give companies a toolkit of ideas from which to choose when putting together their own disaster plans. It is then up to the leaders of the company to prioritize which ideas to put in place and which ideas to ignore based on the specific case of the company. In disaster planning, there is no "one size fits all" solution. Every company is a unique case and must set its priorities accordingly.

CHAPTER 8

THOU SHALT NOT DEPEND ON OTHERS

Human beings are social creatures. We like to help each other and we expect others to help us when we get into trouble. This expectation is fine, but there is a difference between expectation and dependency. It is OK to request help from your peers. It is not OK to plan on it or to be dependent on it. All disaster plans should be written with the expectation that the cavalry will not come and no one will be there to save you. You must plan on being self-sufficient and self-contained.

When Hurricane Katrina hit New Orleans, the local government had a plan in place that called for them to be self sufficient for two days. The thinking was that after 48 hours, the federal government would show up and provide the resources necessary to evacuate the remaining citizens. However, when 48 hours passed, the cavalry had not shown up. In fact, it was a full week before the US Army showed up in sufficient force to take control of the situation, evacuate remaining citizens, and restore law and order to a city overrun with looters and other law breakers.

The lack of competence in the various US government agencies involved in the post-Katrina rescue effort has been well documented. However, the suffering of the people waiting to be evacuated was not simply caused by the incompetence of the federal government. It was also caused by poor planning (or lack of planning) by the local and state governments. The main flaw in the local government's plan was to depend on the federal government to arrive in a timely manner. A more realistic plan would have been to expect to have to be self-sufficient for an extended period of time following the disaster.

In the case of businesses, corporate leaders must understand that their companies must be able to handle disaster management without any help from the government. It is certainly appropriate to ask for help. If the company is lucky, the help may come. It is, however, irresponsible to depend on it. To do so puts employees and corporate assets at risk. This being the case, every disaster plan must assume that no one is coming to help the company.

It is important to note that this does not mean that the company should not ask for help. It should indeed ask for help and generously accept any help that is offered. This may come in the form of some type of bail out (as offered to New York electrical utility Con Edison after 9/11), or in the form of tax breaks and subsidies offered to businesses in New Orleans after Katrina. It may even come from competitors: Financial giant Cantor Fitzgerald received temporary office space from Paine Webber after 9/11. The point here is that the company cannot know exactly what form any public or private assistance might take. This being the case, it is not prudent to plan on it. Also, those companies who are up and running quickly after a disaster will have the opportunity to increase market share gained from their competitors. This is due to the fact that many competitors will be waiting around for assistance, whereas the resilient corporations will be up, running, and providing for their customers.

CHAPTER 9

THOU SHALT KEEP LINES OF COMMUNICATION OPEN

Once a disaster strikes, it is necessary to keep in touch with all employees in order to give everyone instructions on recovery and continued operation of the company. Since disasters tend to break down all regular lines of communication, it is necessary to have alternative lines of communication in place before the disaster strikes so that the company can switch to these communication networks immediately.

When Hurricane Katrina hit the Gulf Coast in 2005, all of the phone lines associated with the New Orleans 504 area code were disabled. This includes both land lines (because the telephone poles were blown down) and cell phones (because the land-line networks and fiber optic cables that the cell phones depend on were flooded.) In the past, conventional wisdom for disaster planners was that all managers simply carried cell phones to communicate with each other. During Katrina, however, any company that depended on cell phones with 504 area codes as their primary means of disaster communication found themselves in great difficulty.

As a result of this lesson, many companies in the Gulf Coast now issue their executives two cell phones: One with the local area code for standard local calls, and a second phone with an area code in another state well outside of the area that could possibly be affected by a Gulf Coast hurricane. This practice assures that executives will be able to communicate regardless of what happens with the local cell phone network.

During Katrina "Communications was the thing that failed everyone," said David Morgan, senior vice president of the Gulf of Mexico Region of P&O Ports Louisiana (Judice, 2006, p. E-2). P&O has invested in two cell phones for each key employee: one for daily use and one with an out of town area code for use during storms. BellSouth is equipping some of its employees on the ground with satellite telephones. Many companies, including Harrah's Casino, have set up toll free numbers out of the region for employees to call for updates during emergencies.

In the year prior to the hurricane, as part of its disaster planning, Peter A. Mayer Advertising, Inc., set up 10 conference call telephone numbers with a telecommunications company outside of the area, and gave one number to each department. After Katrina hit, the numbers allowed each department to have real time meetings with its members, no matter where in the United States they were staying. Mark Mayer, president of the firm, pointed out that the numbers were a more efficient means of communicating than e-mail.

As mentioned in the earlier chapter on redundancy, it is important to have back up computer servers, because an earthquake, hurricane, or terrorist attack will likely shut down the primary server and all e-mail communication with it. In addition to having a back up e-mail server in place, it is prudent to require all employees to provide a personal e-mail address to their department heads in case all internal company systems fail. In fact, it is best for all department heads to maintain a central list (with duplicate copies sent to central management and the emergency planning division) with back up personal phone numbers, e-mail addresses, and close relatives or friends of the employees who could contact them in an emergency. Having all means of potential contact for the employees makes sure that the company will be able to contact them quickly to meet up and get to work as soon as possible after the disruption.

In addition to keeping internal lines of communication open for employees, it is equally important to maintain external lines of communication with distributors, and most importantly, customers. Most companies fail on this count. After a disaster, it is necessary to keep distributors informed as to the status of the company so they will know when to resume shipments. It is more important to keep customers informed so that they will know when they can expect the company to be back on line so that they can come in to get the product or service that they normally get from the company. Those companies that get back on line the quickest, and communicate that they are back on line, will be in a position to capture market share from those companies that do not.

This principle does not only apply to large corporations but to small neighborhood businesses as well. One example is an Irish pub in New Orleans called Finn McCool's. This pub was located in a low lying area of the city and received over ten feet of water during Katrina. It was totally destroyed. The owners, however, intended to rebuild. Rather than leave their customer base in the dark (a serious mistake the vast majority of businesses make all the time), they communicated this intention to their customers right away. They did it through an e-mail distribution list of regular customers that the pub owners had the foresight to collect. Those customers with e-mail could then disseminate the news by word of mouth to those regulars without e-mail.

In addition to informing everyone on the list of their intention to rebuild, they kept the list informed as to the status of the rebuilding as it progressed. They even sent e-mail pictures of the on-going construction so that customers could see the progress with their own eyes. The pub also maintains a web site. When they had their grand re-opening (fittingly on St. Patrick's Day), they were assured of a large turnout since all of their regulars had been kept informed from the beginning. The bar continues to be successful and enjoys a large following of rabidly loyal regulars. In an age where any business, no matter how small, can afford to have an e-mail distribution list and a website to keep customers informed, there is no excuse for any company not to make a small investment in these communication tools. Those companies who refuse to make this investment will do so at their own peril.

CHAPTER 10

THOU SHALT CAPITALIZE ON OPPORTUNITIES

As stated in the first chapter of this text, most companies (and individuals for that matter) fail to adequately prepare for disasters. Conventional wisdom is to wait for the disaster to strike and then figure out how to recover. This is, of course, a bad philosophy. Research (Sheffi, 2006) shows that the most important factor in determining which companies will survive and which ones will not is the steps the organization took in advance to mitigate the disaster, not the steps taken during recovery. Too often, actions taken in the recovery phase are too late and ineffectual. Therefore, it cannot be stressed enough that advance planning is the key. That being said, it is important to successfully execute the recovery process. For those companies who did sufficient preparation in advance, the recovery step will be a chance to capitalize on opportunities and capture market share. For those who did not prepare the first time, the recovery phase is the chance to learn from mistakes and put an effective mitigation plan in place. Once this is done, these companies can also capitalize on opportunities. In either case, the recovery phase is vital to the future of the company and must be executed the same, although the company with a mitigation plan in place before the disruption will, of course, be at an advantage.

After the disaster has passed, the first step is for the company to regroup and communicate with all employees to find out how quickly the company can get back on line. Once the company is back in operation, the next step is to analyze the disaster plan based on the experience of the disaster and to make changes based on what worked last time and what did not work. This way, the disaster plan will be stronger and more effective next time. Of course, if the company did not have a disaster plan before the disruption, now is the time to write one, following the steps outlined in chapter one.

The next step in the recovery process is to search for new opportunities created by the disaster. Every disaster creates opportunities. Most people will fail to realize this. Either opportunities will be created because most competition has been eliminated (due to failure to have or execute an appropriate disaster plan), or opportunities will be created by the disaster itself. However, very few corporations will be a position to capitalize on these opportunities. It is the responsibility of every business leader to not only assure that his or her business survives, but also to assure that the business is positioned to take advantage any opportunities that present themselves. In this way, the business can actually turn tragedy into success.

The first opportunities will come from any government or private assistance offered to businesses after the disruption. Although Commandment Eight argues that a company should not depend on others, accepting assistance is different than dependency. A disaster plan should be put in place that assures that the company can be self-sufficient without regard to outside assistance. This is because there is no guarantee that the outside assistance will come. If the outside assistance does come, there is no way of telling when it will come or what form it will take. So it is better to not plan on it. That being said, it is true after most disasters some form of assistance will be offered. Those corporations that were self sufficient before the assistance kicks in will be well positioned to use the assistance to advance the business and capture market share. Those businesses that were not self-sufficient before the assistance comes will be forced to use the assistance for survival needs. These companies will be at a competitive disadvantage.

For example, after Hurricane Katrina, congress passed a law creating the Gulf Opportunity Zone (The GO Zone) in the area parishes (counties) affected by the storm. The purpose of this act was to encourage economic investment in South Louisiana to help the rebuilding and recovery process. Some of the provisions of the act include: the expanded ability to expense up to 50% of demolition and cleanup costs as well as more time to remediate and expense certain environmental cleanup costs; employee retention and work opportunity tax credits; tax-exempt bond financing available for a limited time to private businesses for office buildings, warehouses, rental housing, manufacturing facilities, shopping centers, retail stores and many other private sector projects; 50% bonus depreciation for new development; the increase in deductions for Section 179 depreciation of new and used personal property used in a trade or business and certain other eligible property; rehabilitation tax credits to restore commercial buildings; and an expanded amount of low-income housing tax credits. Although the specifics of the program are complex, the essence of the program is simple: the government has established a series of financial incentives to reduce business costs and thereby promote investment by the private sector in Louisiana rather than simply embarking on a public building campaign financed solely with public funds. (Although a public building campaign is obviously necessary as well.) This is more cost-effective for the taxpayers, and it is an opportunity for those companies that were correctly positioned before the hurricane.

Real Estate developer Donald Trump was one such person positioned to take advantage of the Go Zone. Donald Trump and his local partners had found a site before the hurricane that was above sea level in one of the high-ground areas of the city. They intended to build a 70 tower hotel and condominium complex that would be able to resist a Category 5 hurricane. During Katrina, the piece of land did not flood, automatically enhancing its value. Also, after Katrina, the Go Zone incentives were put in place, which will actually allow the Trump Organization to reduce its construction costs, thereby increasing its profit margin. The economics work out better for them after Katrina because they had an effective plan in place before Katrina. First, they purchased land on the high ground, planning in advance for possible floods. Second, they had already designed a building that could withstand the winds from a Category 5 Hurricane (an absolute must for commercial real estate in post-Katrina New Orleans), and so they did not have to redesign the building to satisfy potential investors or customers. They had planned for the eventuality of a hurricane even before the building was built. Obviously, very few companies can match the resources of the Trump organization, but regardless of the size of the business, the lesson is the still the same: plan for the worst case scenario and you will be prepared to take advantage of the opportunities that come after a disruption.

In addition to public subsidies that are available to business owners after the storm, another source of opportunity is that the storm creates needs and markets that did not exist before the storm. The opportunities can be taken advantage of by both new businesses created after the storm, as well as pre-existing businesses that carried out different activities before the storm. Recent hurricane recovery efforts have meant billions to upstart businesses. Journalist Seth Borenstein (2006) points out, "If government can't do it, business will. Once the domain of government and charitable relief groups, hurricane response and preparedness are a booming billion dollar business from the self-heating food packets to the souped-up cell phone towers on wheels. Call it hurricane, Inc." (p. E-1). Obviously, those businesses that sell supplies to first responders (satellite phones, generators, tents, etc.) and those that are in the rebuilding business (construction, architecture, and civil engineering firms) have opportunities to do very well after a disaster. However, other types of businesses can capitalize on opportunities if they know where to look and if they know how to recognize those opportunities. For example, after Katrina, there was a large unmet need for laundry facilities. This is not only due the fact that many residents were living in FEMA trailers with no washer and dryer. It is also due to fact that many residents lived in two story houses and their washer and dryer were usually located on the laundry room on the first floor. Even though many of these residents returned to the city after the flood and lived on the second floor of their homes, they had no washer or dyer because most of the houses were in the process of being renovated. This created a large need for laundry facilities. Those laundromats able to repaired and back up into operation quickly after the storm made large profits.

Tourism is the prime industry in the City of New Orleans. Due to fears after the storm, many traditional tourists stopped coming to the city. This put many of the tour guide companies out of business. However, a few tour guide companies figured out how to turn the disaster to their advantage. There were several groups of people who were interested in seeing the disaster up close. Some of them were university groups, some were groups of volunteers from church groups or non-profit groups coming into the city to gut houses or help with the cleanup. Some people were just curious. Whatever the case, there was a group of people interested in seeing the disaster, but who felt they needed a local guide to be safe. The New Orleans "Disaster Tourism" industry was born. Many of the tour companies who specialized in historic tours before the storm now earn large profits giving tours of the areas of the city hardest hit by the hurricane.

Although businesses able to take advantage of a need created after a disaster can make large profits, the primary competitive advantage a resilient business will gain after a disaster is simply the market share it will gain because it is able to get back up and running quicker than its competitors. This was seen in New Orleans. Treasure Chest Casino, a floating casino located in the New Orleans suburb of Kenner, saw its profits rise by over 50 percent after the storm because none of the other casino riverboats in the city were operating, the riverboats on the Mississippi gulf coast had been destroyed, and the land based casino, Harrah's, did not open until six months after the storm. For several months, they were the only game in town, and they benefited because of it. Many shopping malls in suburban New Orleans also reported 50 to 100 increase in sales during the months after Katrina (because the suburbs did not flood as badly as the central city). These malls were well positioned to capture market share. In the final analysis, competitive advantage comes down to being there when your competitors are not.

Conclusion

Resilience is more than just a set of plans and practices. It is a state of mind. Those organizations that are resilient are able to survive and thrive after a disaster primarily because they are led by optimistic human beings who know how to overcome challenges. These individuals are able to instill an all important factor in the organization: a culture of resilience. Culture can be defined here as a set of beliefs, practices, and norms shared by everyone in the organization. MIT Professor Yossi Sheffi (2006), during MIT's three year study on resilient companies and interviews with dozens of companies, found that a culture of resilience was a common element. He argues: "The essence of resilience is the containment of disruption and recovery from it. Culture contributes to resilience by endowing employees with a set of principles regarding the proper response when the unexpected does occur, and when the formal organization's policy does not cover the situation at hand or is too slow to react, it suggests the course of action to take" (p.244).

The purpose of this book is to help organizations instill a culture of resilience into their leadership and employees by offering a simple set of rules that can be understood by everyone in the corporation. These rules are designed to be universal in nature so that they can be applied to any challenge that the organization faces. As stated in the introduction, whenever a company fails after a disaster, inevitably it can be proven that it violated one or more of these commandments. In many ways, the rules expressed here are not simply the hallmarks of a resilient organization, but the hallmarks of an organization that is strong from top to bottom. If the organization is able to put these principles into effect, then not only will they be able to thrive after a disruption, but they will thrive and excel in the regular day to day practice of providing goods and services to customers.

One factor that is absolutely necessary in resilient organizations is strong leadership. A corporation is only as resilient as its leader. A resilient leader will inevitably produce a resilient company. If a leader commits to the ten principles codified in this book, he or she will be able to win the confidence of his or her employees and customers, and be able to lead the organization through any challenge.

The global economy of today is rife with threats and uncertainties: terrorism, earthquakes, tsunamis, hurricanes, heat waves, etc. There is evidence that these disruptions are becoming more frequent as we move forward in time. The reasons are many: international political instability, global warming, the increasing trend to build real estate and settle in vulnerable coastal areas, etc. Whatever the causes may be, the fact remains that disruptions appear to be increasing. In spite of this, most organizations still do not have a systematic plan in place as to how they will survive the next disaster when it comes. And it will come. The organization has no control over the external environment that causes the disruption. The organization has complete control over how it chooses to respond to it. Those organizations who choose to ignore the need to plan and prepare will not survive. Those organizations that choose to prepare for the worst case scenario will not only find they are able to survive during a disruption, but will find that these steps make them a stronger and more efficient organization in the regular day to day marketplace. At the end of the day, the most resilient corporations will also be the most profitable and most able to contribute to society.

References

Bernstein, Amy (2006) Thought Leader: Yossi Sheffi. *Strategy + Business*, Issue 42, Spring, pp. 93–101.

Borenstein, Seth (2006) Hurricane Inc. picks up speed. *The Times Picayune*, April 16, pp. E1, E7.

Colvin, Geoffrey (2005) Value Driven: The Executive Risk Handbook. *Fortune*, October, Vol. 152, No. 7.

Fox, Justin (2005) A Meditation on Risk. *Fortune*, October, Vol. 152, No. 7.

Howell, Donna (2006) Making Sure Disaster Plans Aren't Disasters. *Investors Business Daily,* May 26.

Judice, Mary; King, Ronette; Mowbray, Rebecca; Quillen, Kim; Radtke Russell, Pam; Thomas, Greg; White, Jaquetta. (2006) Battening Down Business. *The Times Picayune*, May 28, Section E, pp. E1, E2.

King, Ronette (2006) Oreck Corp. Expands northward. *The Times Picayune*, July, 25, Section E, pp. C6-C8.

Sheffi, Yossi (2005) The Resilient Enterprise: Overcoming Vulnerability for Competitive Advantage. Cambridge: The MIT Press.

About the Author

Robert A. Collins, Ph.D.

Dr. Robert Collins is Associate Professor of Urban Studies at Dillard University in New Orleans. He has also served as Lecturer in Urban Planning at Harvard University. Prior to his academic career, he was a congressional staff member and served as Field Assistant to U.S. Senator Bennett Johnston. He holds a Ph.D. in Urban Studies from the University of New Orleans. Dr. Collins serves as a speaker, trainer, and consultant to corporations in the areas of strategic planning, risk assessment, and disaster planning.

978-0-595-40924-2
0-595-40924-5